IMAGES OF ENGLAND

CHATHAM
NAVAL DOCKYARD
& BARRACKS

IMAGES OF ENGLAND

CHATHAM
NAVAL DOCKYARD
& BARRACKS

DAVID T. HUGHES

The
History
Press

Frontispiece: Looking from the top of the Main Gate into the dockyard a clear view is gained of the historic Dockyard church.

First published in 2004 by Tempus Publishing
Reprinted 2006

Reprinted in 2009 by
The History Press
The Mill, Brimscombe Port,
Stroud, Gloucestershire, GL5 2QG
www.thehistorypress.co.uk

British Library Cataloguing in Publication Data.
A catalogue record for this book is available from the British Library.

ISBN 978 0 7524 3248 9

Typesetting and origination by
Tempus Publishing Limited.
Printed in Great Britain.

Contents

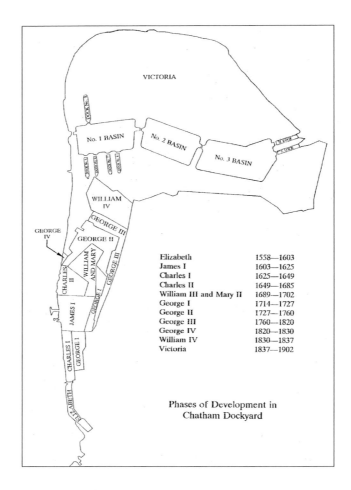

Elizabeth	1558—1603
James I	1603—1625
Charles I	1625—1649
Charles II	1649—1685
William III and Mary II	1689—1702
George I	1714—1727
George II	1727—1760
George III	1760—1820
George IV	1820—1830
William IV	1830—1837
Victoria	1837—1902

Phases of Development in
Chatham Dockyard

Acknowledgements

I would like to thank the several companies and organisations who have supplied information
or photographs, and often both. During my research their staff have responded without
exception to my requests for help with advice and courtesy. They include: Chatham
Dockyard Historical Society, Chatham Historic Dockyard Trust, the *Kent Messenger* Group,
Medway Ports Ltd, Rochester upon Medway Studies Centre and the Royal Engineers'
Library. Thanks must also go to several individuals whose assistance was freely given during
my pursuit of source material. The top of my list in this respect must be Harold Bennett,
CDHS librarian, a veritable fountain of knowledge. Much that is contained within this book
is due to the invaluable assistance of the ever-patient Harold in extracting required material
from his somewhat labyrinthine archives. Also deserving of particular mention for the help
they have given are Maria Clarke, Alison Marsh and Denis O'Neill.

Introduction

Chatham Dockyard owed its inception to King Henry VIII who, in 1547, selected the river Medway at Gillingham to be his main fleet anchorage. On the banks of the river a storehouse was rented for the supplies and equipment necessary for the repair and maintenance of the harboured ships. Soon, further buildings began to appear in close proximity to each other as the fleet's storage requirements increased. Early documents refer to these buildings as being at Gillingham, but they were in fact located slightly up-river, by the water's edge below St Mary's church in the neighbouring parish of Chatham. As more ships were added to the royal fleet, the work of the embryonic dockyard was increased and by 1563, when Queen Elizabeth was on the throne, its expenditure had become more than that of any other royal dockyard. To protect the yard and anchorage from river-borne attack, a small castle, completed in 1564, was built facing across the Medway from Upnor.

Under Elizabeth the dockyard, first officially referred to as Chatham Dockyard in 1567, gained a number of important facilities. The early works included a mast pond dug out in 1570, and a forge and extra storehouses were erected in 1572. In 1580 an ordnance wharf was constructed, complete with a crane for lifting the guns in and out of the ships. The first dry dock was finished in 1581 in order to berth the large galley *Eleanor* and, in 1586, another 'graving place' was made. In 1586, the first Chatham-built naval vessel was launched. This was the *Sunne*, which was a 40 tons, 50ft-long pinnace carrying five guns.

The first serious accident at the dockyard came in the spring of 1591 when the galleon *Revenge*, having been brought up for repair, was lying hulked and unballasted in the river off the yard. When a storm blew up with lashing rain and gale-force winds, the *Revenge*, giving no warning, suddenly rolled over, her keel facing skywards. Strenuous efforts were required before the ship could be righted. A second disaster took place ashore when a three-storey storehouse erected in 1590 was burnt to the ground in 1593.

By the end of Elizabeth's reign in 1603, no other royal dockyard could challenge the supremacy of Chatham, its output being four times as great as all the others combined. From the humble beginnings half a century earlier, a notable establishment had blossomed along 1,000 yards of river bank. The village of Chatham had also grown, and was now a small town, the original handful of villagers' cottages surrounded by a proliferation of hut-like wooden dwellings erected by the incoming dockyard workers.

The continuing expansion of the work load on Chatham was such that in 1618 the building of a large new dockyard began slightly downriver from the original yard. The new establishment was laid out in an approximately rectangular shape, bounded on three sides by ranges of buildings, with riverside wharfage forming the fourth. The south range consisted of the officers' residences and the Main Gate to the yard. The east range, facing the river, incorporated the sail loft and further officers' houses. The north range consisted of storehouses. Since this range ended short of the river, high brick wall was erected from it down to the water's edge. Within the enclosed area a double dock, plus mast ponds, storehouses, workshops and other installations were constructed. A single dock was added in 1623, and a graving dock in the following year. Outside the southern boundary, on part of the land fronting the river between the new and original yards, a large ropery was established. The new yard reached completion in 1626, its predecessor being subsequently relegated to use as a gun wharf and depot.

Attention to the improvement of the building and repair facilities at Chatham was often at the expense of considerations for the workforce who were badly neglected, and the men were sometimes left two years in arrears of their pay. For many of the workers, with their families often near starving, survival had to be sought through the widespread purloining of dockyard stores. During the Civil War the disgruntled men of the yard committed themselves to the Parliamentary cause in the vain hope that their lot would be improved. The disillusioned men would welcome the Restoration in 1660.

When a war broke out with the Dutch in 1664, concern was expressed that Chatham, where the English fleet was laid up in confined waters, was vulnerable to a surprise attack up the Medway. Efforts made to defend the river were dilatory, and the worst fears were realised in June 1667 when a Dutch fleet sailed into the Thames Estuary, attacking and overrunning a still unfinished fort at Sheerness. A squadron of ships then advanced up the Medway, easily riding over a chain placed across the waterway below Gillingham to protect the anchorage. In the ensuing onslaught, several of the finest English vessels were captured or destroyed, the raiders, as they withdrew carrying off with them the *Royal Charles*, flagship of the fleet. Following this humiliation, priority was belatedly given to a major strengthening of the Medway defences.

During the eighteenth century Britain was involved in a number of lengthy wars, during which Chatham Dockyard would be called upon to play its part in maintaining an effective battle fleet. In 1702 Queen Anne became embroiled in an eleven-year war against France, during which time the dockyard underwent a major modernisation with what was effectively a new yard being planned and constructed on the site of the old. A period of peace following Anne's war was broken in October 1739 when a long war broke out with Spain in a clash over colonial interests. France joined the war on the side of Spain in 1744. Wars over colonies meant the Royal Navy having to play a more global role, and the need to keep sufficient ships at sea presented Chatham with a punishing workload. The demands on the yard were not limited to the repair of existing ships. It was also turned into a major shipbuilding centre launching new vessels at an average rate of one a year. By the time of the eventual return to peace in 1763, both men and materials were at the point of exhaustion.

A decade later there would be a great resurgence of activity in the yard as Britain became involved in a long cycle of conflicts involving France as the chief enemy. The dockyard was again hard pressed, its facilities inadequate and outdated for the gruelling output necessary to maintain the war fleets in a battle-ready condition. A major improvement programme was begun with the replacement of many of the old facilities in 1785. The new ropery and the Anchor Wharf storehouses are among the surviving buildings from this period of renewal. All the efforts to keep an effective navy at sea would be justified by events. As the wars continued, the destruction of Europe's three naval powers, Holland, France and Spain, gave Britain complete command of the sea. After the return to peace in 1815 the fleets of the Royal Navy would remain supreme on every ocean until the next century.

David T. Hughes
August 2004

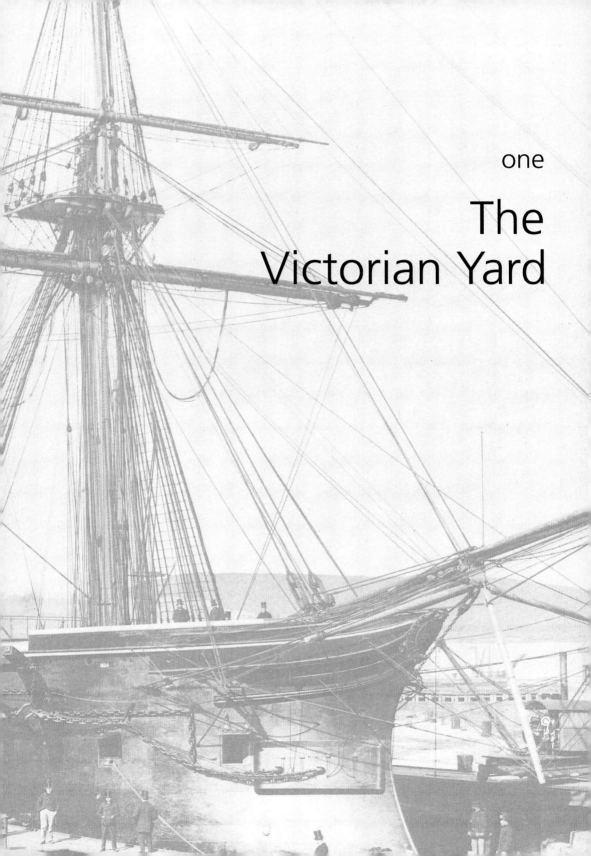

one

The Victorian Yard

Queen Victoria's reign commenced in 1837 and would last for over sixty years. During that period the Royal Navy was to witness some of the most profound changes that had yet occurred in ship design. Steam would supplant sail as the means of propulsion, iron and later steel would replace wood as the main construction material, and for weaponry the broadsides of muzzle-loaded cannon would be superseded by rotating gun turrets and breech-loaded ordnance with rifled barrels that fired high explosive shells. At Chatham the wind of change began to blow in September 1832, when its first steam-driven vessel, the six-gun paddle-sloop *Phoenix*, was launched. Within the dockyard the use of steam power had already taken root and was being found in increasingly widespread applications. With the new technologies came new trades and challenging changes among the traditional ones. When the building of the *Achilles*, Chatham's first iron warship, began in 1863, boilermakers were contracted in to carry out her plating. When these men subsequently went on strike over pay they were dismissed. In a major departure from their traditional skills, the dockyard shipwrights then agreed to take over the work, switching to working mainly in iron (and later steel) instead of wood. Chatham's first steel-built ship, the corvette *Calypso*, was launched in June 1883. From 1876 onwards, electrical power became increasingly utilised on board the ships and within the dockyards. All electrical work at Chatham was carried out by the constructive department shipfitters, until 1903 when an electrical department was established.

Access to the dockyard was through an impressive early Georgian gateway which had a large royal coat of arms in coloured relief above its archway.

The Dockyard church. Along the road to the left, the heads of the No.1 and No.2 covered slipways are visible. No.1 Slip had its roof removed and was filled in during 1892. At the same time No.2 Slip was also filled in, but its roof survived until it was destroyed by fire in 1966.

Above: Shipwrights at work fitting out the gun deck of the new frigate *Euryalus* which was launched at Chatham on 5 October 1854. A decade later they would, for the first time, be working in iron as well as their traditional wood.

Right: No.2 Covered Dock undergoing lengthening in 1856. The dock was originally built in 1623 and was the site of the building of Chatham's most famous ship, the *Victory*, which was floated out in 1765.

No.3 Covered Slipway. Starting life as a dock in 1686, it was converted to a slipway in 1830, and its timber covering was added in 1838.

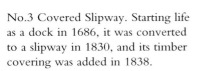

Medway House – as it became known after 1970 – was the official residence of the chief executive officer of the dockyard. It was built at the beginning the eighteenth century as accommodation for the Resident Commissioner at Chatham. Following a reorganisation of naval administration in 1832 it became the house of the Superintendent of the dockyard.

The rear of Medway House, seen from its extensive walled garden in 1857. The three-storied plum-coloured brick building, a fine example of Queen Anne architecture, remains extant as the oldest dockyard building in the country.

Captain-Superintendent George Goldsmith with his wife by the fountain in the garden of Medway House, 1857. The garden had contained a fountain for many years. One is known to have existed in the Commissioner's garden the end of the seventeenth century.

This picture shows the entrance to the large 350ft-long Ordnance Storehouse at the Gun Wharf, standing on the site of the original Tudor Dockyard. The Gun Wharf was not just a depot of heavy ordnance; the stores included a substantial arsenal of cutlasses, rifles, pistols and other hand-held weapons.

The northern end of the Ordnance Storehouse in 1855 with the Storekeeper's House in the foreground. Out of sight in the foreground was a large open storage area tightly packed with gun barrels for heavy ordnance.

Eighteenth-century sheds, erected over the side of one of the mast ponds, viewed in around 1856. There were two similar rows of sheds: one, over the northern end of the South Mast Pond, being used as a mast store while the other, over the northern side of the North Mast Pond, was utilised as a boat store.

The *Wellesley*, with seventy-four guns, became guardship of the *Ordinary* at Chatham in 1862, but was shortly afterwards commissioned as a training ship for boys. In 1866 she resumed her duties as guardship until loaned to the School Ship Training Society in 1868 and removed to Purfleet.

The battleship *Achilles*, whose keel was laid down in No.2 Dock on 1 August 1863, was the first iron ship built in the yard.

The *Achilles* as her construction was approaching completion. She would have two engines to drive her single propeller with an output power of 5,720hp.

The *Achilles* was launched on 23 December 1863. Her complement was 450. Although steam-engined, with bunkers for 750 tons of coal, she also carried 50,000sq ft of canvas on her three masts.

The battleship *Bellerophon* in No.3 Dock. Her keel was laid down on 23 December 1863 and her launching ceremony, when she was floated out, took place on 26 May 1865.

A depiction of the accident in the Steam Hammer Workshop on 7 September 1866. Shortly after the start of the working day a large boiler, which could operate at a pressure of 60lb/sq in, suddenly blew up. As a result of the explosion two workmen were killed and several more were injured.

Large pieces of the boiler were thrown into the air, including its top, weighing around 7 tons, which landed in the passage between the Foundry and the Smithery. Adjacent buildings were seriously damaged, including the Boiler House and part of the Foundry.

The *Atlas* moored as a hulk in the river Thames at Long Reach, having been lent to the Metropolitan District Asylum Board as a hospital ship in 1884. The *Atlas* had been launched at Chatham on 21 July 1860 as a ninety-one gun warship. She was eventually sold to be broken up in 1904.

two

The Great Extension

By the early years of Queen Victoria's reign the ever-expanding size and number of ships in the Royal Navy was leading to a major shortage of dockyard facilities. Of the Royal Yards giving access to the North Sea, only Chatham was regarded by the Admiralty as having potential for development to provide significantly increased docking and repair capabilities. The only direction still open to expansion was downriver towards a loop in the river intersected across its neck by a narrow channel – St Mary's Creek – to form a D-shaped island of marshland known as St Mary's Island. In anticipation of an enlargement of the dockyard, 19 acres adjoining the northern extremity of the yard was bought by the Crown in 1847, and by the purchase of an additional 185 acres in 1854, the whole of St Mary's Island was acquired. Responsibility for planning the layout and construction of the extension lay with the Corps of Royal Engineers. Convict labour gangs were to be widely used for the construction of the new facilities. Preliminary work began in 1855, the river wall being extended northwards to the entrance to St Mary's Creek, and part of the island embanked. The most ambitious part of the project then commenced. This was the conversion of the creek into a chain of three interlinked basins, each 700ft wide, with dry-docking facilities provided in the western basin. Twenty years after the work had begun the extension was completed, and the official opening took place on 26 September 1885.

In order to house the convicts working on the extension, a prison – St Mary's Prison – was built between 1854 and 1856 on part of the site where the Royal Navy Barracks would later stand. In all there were about 1,700 prisoners and an official prison staff of 232, including 117 armed warders. The prison was demolished in 1898.

Adjacent to the prison stood the Prison Governor's House. The Governor presided over a prison administration which subjected the inmates to a harsh regime where even relatively minor infringements of the regulations could be punished by solitary confinement on bread and water.

Beyond the northern corner of the dockyard lay the large area of marshy ground, containing St Mary's Creek and Island, which was to be used for the new extension.

The Site Office erected on St Mary's Island for the engineers overseeing the works. Colonel Charles W. Pasley, RE, Superintending Civil Engineer, and Mr Edward A. Bernays, Civil Engineer, supervised the work carried out by convict labour, and later by the hired men initially employed by Mr Gabrielli, the Contractor.

Looking westwards across the northern section of St Mary's Island is the landing jetty that was erected so that materials brought to the construction works by sailing vessel could be off-loaded.

Bricks required for the new works were manufactured on site. To this end, the laying of a large brickfield had begun in 1865 in a rectangular area occupying approximately 21 acres. It was anticipated that the required brick earth would be provided from the excavation works centred on St Mary's Creek.

This picture shows convicts unloading a barge containing raw materials for the brickworks. Blue gault clay was brought in from Burham and yellow sand from Aylesford to be mixed with the brick earth found on site, which turned out to be of inferior quantity and present in much smaller quantities than anticipated.

The Hacks: storage units for drying the moulded bricks before baking. The average output from the brickfields would be over 23,000 bricks a week, the majority of which were used in the construction of the walls of the basins. By March 1875 the total number of bricks manufactured had reached 110 million.

One of the brick kilns at the dockyard extension. The first bricks left the new kilns on 26 March 1866. Having been baked at a temperature of 1,000 °C the result was a high quality reddish-brown brick resembling terracotta in texture.

This image shows one of the coffer dams constructed to seal off the two ends of St Mary's Creek which was tidal, allowing it to be drained. Lock gates would be constructed at the river entrances so that the water in the basins could be maintained at a consistent level.

A line of pile drivers. Large numbers of timber piles were driven 60ft deep into the marshy ground to provide stable foundations for the walls of the intended basins and dry docks.

Excavated earth was removed from the site of the basins on tramways. The earth was spread over the surrounding low lying marshland which thus raised the ground level to an average height of 6ft above the high water mark of a normal spring tide.

The travelling crane used for moving the blocks of masonry shipped in for use on the works. Portland stone quarried by convicts was used, being employed in the construction of the dry docks and to face the walls of the basins above the neap tide water level.

A section of a basin wall under construction. The lower level consisted of a concrete wall faced with brickwork, hoop iron being used between the courses, while the whole the top section was built entirely of brickwork with the uppermost portion, above water level, faced with stone.

Aerial view of the completed works looking westwards across the three basins, 1960s. In the foreground is No.3 (Fitting Out) Basin with the two lock gates. Behind it lies the No.2 (Factory) Basin and, in the distance is the No.1 (Repairing) Basin. Together, the basins occupied over 68 acres.

three

Apprentices

In the traditional mode of dockyard apprenticeship the apprentice was indentured to a master, often his own father, who received his wages and was responsible for his upkeep as well as instructing him in the skills of his trade. This scheme gave no guarantee that an apprentice would receive proficient training. To improve the system a radical change was introduced in 1801 by which every future apprentice was instead indentured to the principal officer of his trade who would then allocate him to a competent craftsman for instruction. By the reign of Queen Victoria the Admiralty was also concerned that those entering apprenticeships were insufficiently educated to cope with the theoretical principles of the new technologies that were permeating into shipbuilding practice. To remedy this, a dockyard school was established in 1843, the first custom-built schoolhouse being completed in 1847. An apprentice's progress through the school was determined by internally set examinations until National Certificate Courses were introduced in 1952. At the same time the school was re-designated 'Chatham Dockyard Technical College'. The college accommodation, having become overcrowded, was relocated at Collingwood, which was formerly part of the Royal Naval Barracks, in the summer of 1960. In the autumn the apprentice group training centres for the fitter trades were also centralised in Collingwood. The dockyard college was eventually closed for economical reasons in July 1971, apprentices having thenceforth to attend courses in local further education colleges.

The original dockyard school building, lying in the shadow of the dockyard wall. The main entrance to the school was the less than imposing door on the right.

The engine fitter apprentice training centre. In 1942 the first group training centres had been established in the dockyard for the first and second year engine fitter apprentices. The training centre was relocated to Collingwood in 1960.

The entrance to the Collingwood centre. The iron gates carried the badges of the dockyard and the dockyard college. Collingwood Barracks dated from 1932 when they had been built as a mechanical training establishment for royal naval artificer apprentices.

The apprentice group training centre for the first- and second-year fitter apprentices was situated in the East Wing, or Rodney Block, at Collingwood.

Engine fitter apprentices under group instruction in the Refit Section at the Collingwood training centre, being trained to strip down, refurbish and reassemble pumps, condensers, turbines and other engineering units.

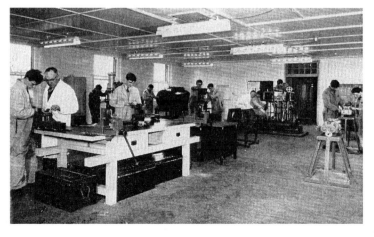

Shipwright apprentices in their training centre at the boat house completing a 14ft dinghy in 1964. The building of a dinghy, which was afterwards tested in one of the dockyard basins, was for many years an integral part of the shipwrights' training.

Boilermaker apprentices receiving instruction in 1981. Group training was not available for the smaller trades, such as sailmakers, smiths and painters, that only entered one or two apprentices a year.

The Dockyard Technical College, housed in the West Wing at Collingwood, where it had been relocated in 1960.

A technical drawing lecture in progress in the college. During term time, apprentices attended the college once a week on a day-release basis.

The college library at Collingwood. A part of the Nore Command library was transferred to the college on the closure of the Nore Command in 1961. The college library had nearly 10,000 volumes and received regular additions to its reference and fiction sections.

In April 1969 a change in the regulations allowed girls to compete in the apprentice entrance examinations. In 1971 Zandra Bradley, the first ever girl apprentice at Chatham, was entered as an electrical fitter apprentice.

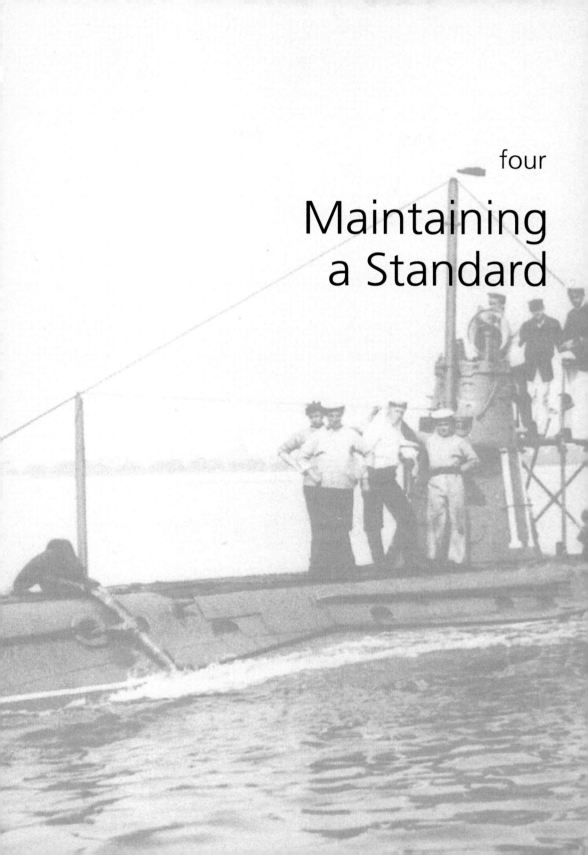

four

Maintaining
a Standard

Britain's naval supremacy at the dawn of the twentieth century was upheld by the adoption of the two-power standard by which the Royal Navy was maintained at a strength at least equal to that of the combined fleets of any other two maritime powers. However, this arrangement had come under mounting stress from an unexpected quarter. An increasingly militant Germany, impatient to expand its interests abroad, had noted that the strength of the Royal Navy had been the key factor in both the establishment and maintenance of Britain's world dominance. It decided therefore, that a powerful navy was essential to the furtherance of German's global ambitions and a major shipbuilding programme was begun to transform the country's small coastal defence force into a large ocean-going navy. As the new German warships followed each other down the slipways, Britain viewed the challenge to its naval strength with considerable alarm and began the construction of a series of new capital ships in order to maintain the traditional balance of power. This would result in the country becoming locked into a great naval arms race. Chatham found itself working at full capacity to fulfil its part in a spiralling navy building programme. By 1903 the number of employees has swollen to 10,000. A small but growing number of these were women, the door being prised open to them a little more on 28 March 1905 when the first seven women tracers with their own charge woman were admitted to drawing office staff.

Looking across the Medway towards the Upnor-facing entrance of the dockyard basins in the early years of the twentieth century. New vessels launched from the riverside slipways would be brought in through this entrance for completion.

A small forest of masts and funnels belonging to the warships docked in No.3 Basin. They represented a minute proportion of the huge armada of vessels that made up Britain's naval might.

No.8 Slip, commenced in 1897 and completed in 1900. It was constructed to give Chatham the capacity to build the increasingly large warships being ordered by the navy. Production of the largest class of battleships, the dreadnoughts, would continue to be beyond Chatham's scope.

A punching machine at work in 1901. It is producing rivet holes in a ship's plate that is to be used on the *Prince of Wales*, a battleship in the process of construction on No.7 Slip.

Left: The *Prince of Wales* having hull plating added during the latter stages of her construction. She was launched by Mary, Princess of Wales, on 25 March 1902. By an order of that year, in future all naval warships would be painted grey so they would be camouflaged. The *Prince of Wales* was commissioned at Chatham on 18 May 1904.

Below: While at Chatham for the launch of the *Prince of Wales*, the Prince and Princess of Wales formally opened a dockyard museum that had been established on the first floor of a large shed situated between Nos 2 and 3 Docks. Here, the large collection of ships' figureheads are on display.

Opposite below: The Mould Loft Building was gutted by a fire on the morning of 6 June 1902. The building, with the mould loft on the upper floor and drawing offices on the ground floor, had been opened in 1885. All the drawings and records were lost in the fire. The building was subsequently repaired and put back into use.

Above: A naval working party leaving the storehouse in the Clock Tower Building with a consignment of rope and other supplies which are being carried on the dockyard railway by the engine *Khartum*. The roof over No.2 Dock is in the background.

No.8 Machine Shop situated on the east side of No.8 Dock. The building was originally the structure, completed in 1845, to provide a roof over a building slip at Woolwich Dockyard. When that dockyard closed in 1869 the roof was dismantled and brought to Chatham where it was re-erected in 1880 as a machine shop.

Torpedo Fitting Shop, c.1905. The Royal Navy first adopted the Whitehead torpedo in 1869. By the twentieth century it was an essential part of the weaponry of all capital ships, and had also led to a new class of vessel, the torpedo gunboat.

Women in the ropery spinning hemp for the manufacture of ships' cables, *c.*1902. The first women workers in the dockyard were those employed by the ropery and colour loft in 1866.

Women sewing flags in the colour loft, *c.*1902. By this time sewing machines, belt driven from an overhead pulley shaft, had been introduced for carrying out the majority of the work previously stitched by hand.

Men gathering to receive their wages on pay day. The dockyard work hours during summer time were from 7.00a.m. to 12.00p.m., and from 1.30p.m. to 5.30p.m. On Saturdays work in the dockyard ended at midday.

No.3 Muster Station. Each employee was issued with a hexagonal brass tally bearing his name and number. Having arrived for work he would deposit this in a tally box at his allocated Muster Station, retrieving it during the out-muster. Those who were late for work would find the tally box locked and would suffer a loss of wages.

Pembroke Gate, giving access to the northern section of the yard, had since the building of the great extension with its basins and workshops formed the dockyard's busiest place of entry and exit.

Trams waiting outside Pembroke Gate for the rush of homeward-bound men that followed each out-muster. The tram service was inaugurated on 17 June 1902, initially operating on a single route which ran from Pembroke Gate via Chatham Town Hall to the outlying district of Luton. The trams, which proved a great boon to the dockyard men, eventually stopped running and were replaced by buses in September 1930.

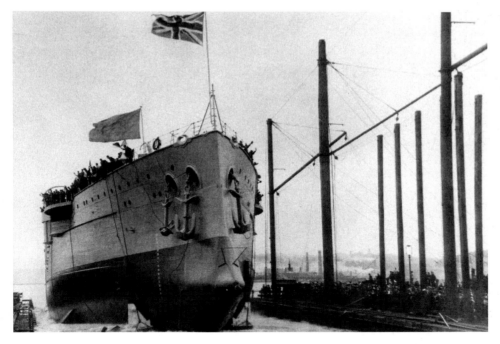

The battleship *Africa* being launched from No.8 Slip following her christening by the Marchioness of Londonderry on 20 May 1905. She was the last battleship to be constructed at Chatham and also, at 16,350 tons displacement, the largest ship to be built at the yard.

The A.1 which in 1911 became the first submarine to be refitted at Chatham. Following the introduction of submarines by the Admiralty, Chatham was the first Royal Naval Dockyard to specialise in this new kind of vessel. The A.1 had been involved in an unfortunate accident in 1904 when she was in a collision with the SS *Berwick Castle* and sank. She was raised and put back into service.

The first steam–turbine–powered ship built at Chatham, the cruiser *Chatham*, was launched from No.8 Slip on 9 November 1911.

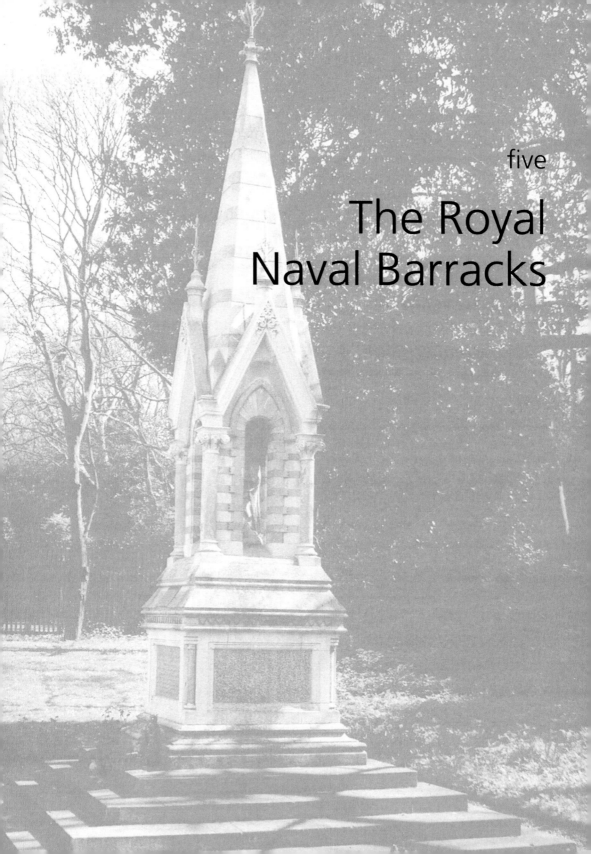

five

The Royal
Naval Barracks

The Royal Naval Depot was founded in 1890 aboard three hulks alongside the south wall of No.2 Basin. These hulks were the *Pembroke*, *Royal Adelaide* and *Forte*. Within a few years these were replaced by a shore base, the Royal Naval Barracks, designated the name HMS *Pembroke*. Construction of these barracks began in May 1897 and they were completed in 1902. The barracks were officially opened on 30 April 1903 when, with the Depot Band at their head, the officers and men marched from the hulks out of the dockyard in through the Main Gate of their new home. In the decades that followed several new facilities were added to the barracks. By the 1960s, however, with the gradual reduction in size of the Royal Navy, as Britain abandoned its worldwide commitments, the barracks had begun to run down, parts being taken over by the dockyard, including the Drill Shed and Canteen. Following the ending of the Nore Command in March 1961 the barracks were used as an accommodation centre for the crews of ships refitting in the yard and to house the Royal Naval Supply School which gave naval personnel training in supply and secretarial work. In 1970 it was announced that all naval establishments at Chatham, including the dockyard and *Pembroke*, were being combined together as a single establishment to be known as HM Navy Base, commanded by a single naval officer bearing the title Flag Officer Medway and Port Admiral. In 1984 the barracks would finally close as part of a government decision to sweep away all remaining naval presence on the Medway.

The main entrance to the Naval Barracks, situated at the bottom end of Dock Road, gave access at the western end of the barracks.

The three accommodation hulks of the Naval Depot – *Pembroke*, *Royal Adelaide* and *Forte* – alongside the south wall of No.2 Basin. The *Pembroke* had started life as the *Duncan*, with 101 guns, before becoming the main accommodation hulk at Chatham in 1890.

The new Royal Naval Barracks which, at the time of its opening, could accommodate 4,742 officers and men.

The first ceremonial port divisions being held on the parade ground of the new barracks in 1903.

The Officers' smoking room, situated in the Wardroom Block which offered some palatial surroundings compared with the cramped conditions aboard the *Pembroke* hulk.

The Engine Room Artificers' mess likewise presented some spacious luxury after the low deckheads and dingy compartments of the former accommodation aboard the hulk.

A barrack room in one of the accommodation blocks. Emulating shipboard conditions, barrack rooms were organised into messes. There were a dozen messes in each room; each mess comprised fourteen men with their own table and benches. The men were required to sleep in hammocks.

The Drill Shed flanking the northern side of the parade ground. During the First World War this would be used as additional dormitory accommodation.

The interior of the Drill Shed. One night in 1917, while the shed was being used as a temporary wartime barracks, it was bombed from an enemy aircraft, killing 135 sleeping ratings and injuring many more.

The swimming pool. The barracks also boasted a large gymnasium, and both this and the swimming pool were used to train the men and for recreational purposes.

The garrison church, dedicated to St George, had its foundation stone laid in 1905. Upon completion in 1906 the building was dedicated by the Bishop of Rochester.

The ornate interior of St George's church looking eastwards towards the altar. The walls of the church were adorned with memorials to the men of the Chatham Port Division who had lost their lives during the two world wars.

The bodies of French Prisoners of War and their memorial were removed from St Mary's Island in 1909 and relocated in the barracks adjacent to the church.

The six original accommodation blocks were all named after famous British Admirals: Anson, Blake, Duncan, Grenville, Hawke and Nelson. Six decades later a new addition, Mountbatten Block, was added at their eastern end.

The final port divisions to be held at Pembroke Barracks before their closure. The White Ensign was lowered in the barracks for the last time on 17 February 1984.

six

Building
Submarines

During the last quarter of the nineteenth century an American, John P. Holland, had been successful in developing an efficient class of submarine craft. Due to traditional naval conservatism there were many in the Royal Navy unwilling to see the introduction of submarines. Admiral Sir Arthur K. Willson had described them as 'underhand, unfair and damned un-English', advocating that any captured enemy submarine crews should be hanged as pirates. However, in 1900 the Admiralty, noting that other major maritime powers were not being so reticent about acquiring submarines, decided to press forward with an order for the new craft and, between 1902 and 1903, five Holland type submarines were built for the navy by Messrs Vickers at Barrow. Improved versions – the A and B classes – followed swiftly, and these in turn were superseded from 1906 by the superior C class. It was with the construction of C-class submarines that Chatham first came into the picture as a submarine building yard. Six C-class submarines were built in rapid succession at Chatham, the first British submarines to be launched outside Barrow embarking the dockyard on a long era of specialisation in submarine construction. The first Chatham submarine, the C.17, was launched from No.7 Slip on 13 August 1908. Between 1908 and 1967, Chatham would construct a total of fifty-seven submarines, among which the X.1, E.1, F.1, G.1, R.1, *Oberon*, *Parthian* and *Swordfish* would be the prototypes for a succession of class types. The *Oberon*, launched on 24 August 1926, would be the first submarine to be given a name rather than carrying just a class letter and number.

No.7 Slip quickly became established as Chatham's specialist building slip for the construction and launching of submarines.

The C.17 (280 tons), the first submarine to be built at Chatham, was launched from No.7 Slip on 13 August 1917. She possessed a petrol engine which gave her 16 knots on the surface, an electric motor which produced 10 knots submerged, and was armed with two 18in torpedo tubes.

The submarine E.1, launched at Chatham on 9 November 1912, was the first of six E-class submarines to be built in the dockyard. They had diesel engines and carried four 18in torpedo tubes.

Above: The submarine cruiser X.1, launched on 16 June 1923, was, at 2,780 tons, the largest submarine constructed at Chatham. She packed a heavy punch, her armaments including four 5.2in guns mounted in twin turrets, and six 21in torpedo tubes.

Left: The *Seahorse* in the Medway following her launch on 15 November 1932. The men in the small boats are collecting wax from the river's surface. This wax had been used as lubricant on the slipways to enable the submarine to slide smoothly into the river.

The *Starfish* following the launch by Mrs S.O. Summers, Mayoress of Gillingham, 14 March 1933.

The frames of the *Grampus*, a mine-laying submarine, under construction on the building slip in 1934. She was launched in February 1936.

The *Umpire* was launched at Chatham on 30 December 1940. One of the U-class vessels designed to be unarmed training submarines, with the outbreak of war four torpedo tubes were hurriedly incorporated into her construction. She is on her builder's trials at Chatham in June 1941.

The *Turpin* was launched by Lady Tovey, wife of Admiral of the Fleet, Lord Tovey, on 5 August 1944. *Turpin*'s cradle being returned up the slipway after the launch.

Crowds gathered on 18 July 1959 for the launching ceremony of the *Oberon*, first of the Oberon-class submarines, generally referred to within the yard as O-boats.

Watched by a large number of spectators gathered at No.7 Slip, the *Oberon* is christened by Princess Marina, Duchess of Kent.

The *Oberon*'s first commanding officer, Lt–Com. J.F. Merewether, addresses the assembled crowd at the submarine's commissioning ceremony, which took place on the north side of No.2 Basin on 9 February 1961.

Dockyard officials and members of the *Oberon*'s ship's company gathered on her casing for a commissioning day photograph. She carried sixty-eight men as her seagoing complement.

The *Ocelot* was the final submarine built at Chatham for the Royal Navy. She is moving down the slipway towards the Medway at her launch on 5 May 1962. In 1991 she was sold to the Chatham Historic Trust for conservation and now remains on permanent display at Chatham.

In January 1964, just a few weeks before the *Ojibwa* – the first of three Oberon-class submarines to be built for the Royal Canadian Navy – was launched, the surrounding slipway was cleared as she underwent final preparations.

Shipwright caulkers pouring wax, liquified by heating, onto the ways where it would solidify to present a low-friction sliding surface. The launch of the *Ojibwa* was carried out on 29 February 1964.

Her post-launch fitting-out completed, the commissioning ceremony of the *Ojibwa* took place in No.3 Basin on 23 September 1965.

The *Onondaga*, the second of the submarines to be built for the Canadians, having been brought round into No.8 Dock following her launch on 25 September 1965.

The final submarine to be built at Chatham was the *Okanagan*. She is moving down the slipway towards the river at her launching on 17 September 1966. The submarine was formally handed over to the Royal Canadian Navy on 22 June 1968.

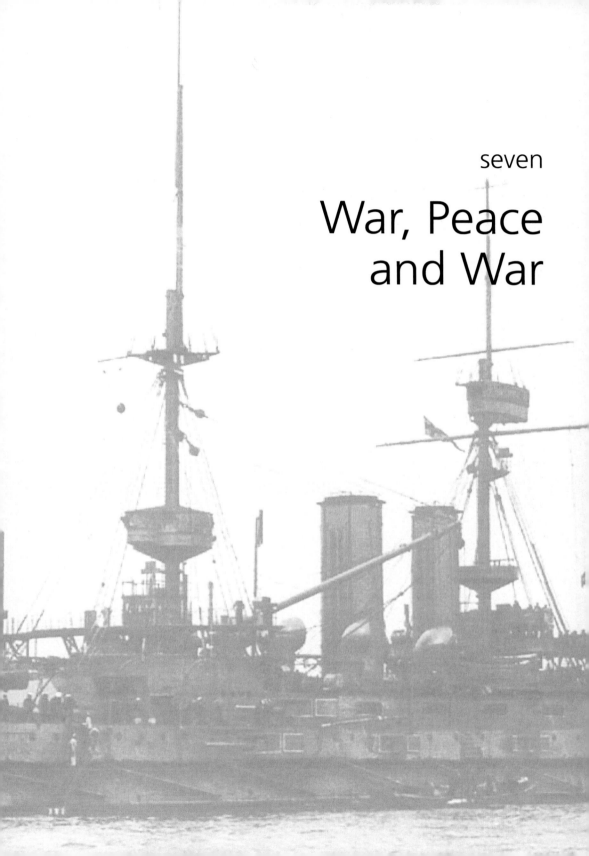

seven

War, Peace and War

During the two world wars, Chatham Dockyard found itself working on a twenty-four hour schedule to cope with the large numbers of ships coming in damaged in action or needing major servicing. For the first time, the yard became the target for enemy bombers. Just after 11.00p.m. on 3 September 1917, four German night-raiders attacked the yard, one bomb achieving a direct hit on the R.N. Barracks, leaving 135 ratings dead and a further 88 injured. The first decade of the inter-war years was an unsettled period for the yard. Much of the swollen workforce recruited into the yard during the war was made redundant as the workload subsided to peacetime levels and the many workmen called into the armed forces returned to reclaim their old jobs. As the whole country began to slump into depression and economic crisis, further employees found themselves out of work. By the mid-thirties the situation was about to rapidly improve. The rising spectre of another war with Germany had led the government to introduce what would prove to be an accelerating process of rearmament, with many existing ships undergoing modernisation and also the inception of a new building programme. Once again employment in the yard began to climb, and it was working at maximum capacity by the time the Second World War broke out in 1939.

On the morning of 26 November 1914, the battleship *Bulwark* was lying downriver from Chatham at Kethole Reach, taking in ammunition. Suddenly there was a tremendous explosion as her magazines accidentally detonated. Only a handful of her crew of over 780 survived.

On 26 May 1915, the minelayer *Princess Irene* was moored in the Medway, not far from the scene of the *Bulwark* disaster. Suddenly she too blew up as her cargo of mines detonated, caused, it was afterwards suspected, by a faulty arming device being inserted into one of the mines. More than 170 crew and 76 Sheerness dockyard workers were killed. A naval stoker was the single survivor.

The tribal class destroyer *Nubian*, after being torpedoed by a German destroyer off the Belgian coast and losing her bow section on 27 October 1916.

The *Zulu*, also a tribal class destroyer, was struck by a mine in the Dover Straits on 8 November and had her stern blown off. On 26 April 1917 the undamaged sections of the *Nubian* and *Zulu* were placed in No.7 Dock at Chatham, emerging joined together as the destroyer *Zubian* on 7 June.

The cruiser *Vindictive* had been launched at Chatham on 9 December 1897. At the beginning of 1918 she was back in Chatham being fitted with a false deck and heavily armed for the famous Zeebrugge raid on 23 April, where under withering enemy fire she disembarked landing parties on the heavily defended mole.

The cruiser *Kent* was launched from No.8 Slip at Chatham on 16 June 1926. Although, at 9,850 tons, she was not the heaviest warship built in the dockyard, her dimensions of 590ft overall and 68¼ft beam made her the longest and largest, and the slip had to be lengthened for her construction.

The cruiser *Euryalus* was launched from No.8 Slip on 6 June 1939. War had broken out by the time she was commissioned in 1941, and she would serve in both the Pacific and Mediterranean theatres of operation.

Above: Bomb damage to the compressor house in 1942. During the war a total of 92 high-explosive and over 2,000 incendiary bombs fell on the dockyard. The most serious incident occurred on 3 December 1940 when a bomb which fell on the factory killed eight workers and injured sixty-three others.

Right: The German submarine U 570 was disabled by a RAF Hudson bomber and abandoned in the North Sea on 27 August 1941. She was taken in tow by RN vessels and recommissioned as HMS *Graph* in September 1941. She is undergoing repair in No.3 Basin at Chatham, early in 1944.

The submarine *Graph*, ex-German U-boat U 570, in dry dock at Chatham. Following her repairs, she is here having her hull cleaned and repainted before being put back into service.

The double launch of the sloops *Modeste* and *Nereide* from No.8 Slip on 29 January 1944. They were built to be deployed on escort duties, but the war had ended by the time of their completion.

eight

Visiting Royalty

During the first 150 years of its existence, several of the reigning monarchs would make visits to their dockyard at Chatham. Elizabeth I made her visit in 1581. Her successor, James I, made two visits in 1604 and 1606 respectively while his son, Charles I, was at the dockyard in 1631. The Duke of York (later James II) was very familiar with the yard and anchorage at Chatham. He was a skilled sailor who in 1660 commanded the squadron that brought his brother (Charles II) back from exile in France. Following the Restoration he was created Lord High Admiral. The first Hanoverian kings showed little interest in their navy or dockyards but Prince William, Duke of Clarence (later William IV – 'The Royal Tar'), would serve between 1779 and 1828 as a professional sailor, nearly eleven years of this time being spent on active service at sea. Over the next 200 years, many members of the Royal family served in the Royal Navy. Prince Alfred, Duke of Edinburgh, the second son of Queen Victoria, was a career sailor. He entered the Royal Navy in 1858 and became an Admiral of the Fleet in 1893. When he died in 1899 he had spent over forty years in the navy. During the next century three monarchs – George V, Edward VIII and George VI – served in the navy, as would Prince Charles between 1971 and 1976. It was a century that would witness a number of visits from the various members of the Royal family to the chief naval establishments in Chatham and the surrounding area.

Princess Alexandra, Princess of Wales (later Queen Alexandra) 'christened' the ironclad battleship *Alexandra* at Chatham Dockyard on 7 April 1875. A crowd of over 25,000 watched as the ship was launched into the Medway. The Princess's husband (the future Edward VII) was present with her on the launch platform.

Prince Alfred, Duke of Edinburgh, presented new colours to the Chatham Division of the Royal Marines on 22 June 1896. Prince Alfred (centre), the Royal Marines' Honorary Colonel, standing with divisional officers outside the Royal Marines Officers' Mess.

On 26 July 1905 Edward VII opened the new Royal Naval Hospital at Chatham. Having carried out the opening ceremony he made a tour of inspection of the hospital's facilities. He is seen departing the hospital in the royal carriage.

George V inspecting Marines during a wartime 'morale boosting' visit in April 1918. The King walked from the dockyard to the Royal Marine Barracks, inspecting members of the Chatham Division Royal Marines along the way.

The King meeting some of the 11,300 men employed as dockyard workers at Chatham during the First World War.

The King being driven past some of the 1,000 women employed in the dockyard during the First World War. The war was the first time that women had been employed in such numbers in the dockyard, though they had been employed in the production of both rope and flags for many years.

On 26 April 1924 Edward, Prince of Wales (the future Edward VIII) was in Chatham to unveil a memorial to those lost from the Chatham Division of the Royal Navy during the First World War. There were more than 30,000 spectators present to witness the occasion.

Left: Prince George, Duke of Kent, inspecting a parade of naval ratings during a visit to the Medway Towns in the summer of 1931. He would be killed on active service in 1942.

Right: Queen Elizabeth made a wartime visit to the members of the Nore Command of the WRNS in May 1941. She is being met by Third Officer Hollands, WRNS.

George VI made a 'secret' wartime visit to naval personnel in the Medway Towns on 16 April 1942. Due to wartime security restrictions, the King's visit was only made public after it had occurred. His Majesty is seen here undertaking an inspection of naval ratings in HMS *Pembroke*.

Above: On 12 July 1948 George VI paid a second visit to inspect the naval establishments at Chatham. All along the route between his various ports of call crowds were gathered to cheer as he passed.

Right: At the dockyard a shipwright apprentice, Denis O'Neill, stands proudly to attention in the line-up of dockyard employees selected to be introduced to the King.

The King inspecting Sea Cadet Corps cadets, who are aged from nine to thirteen, on the parade ground in Pembroke Barracks.

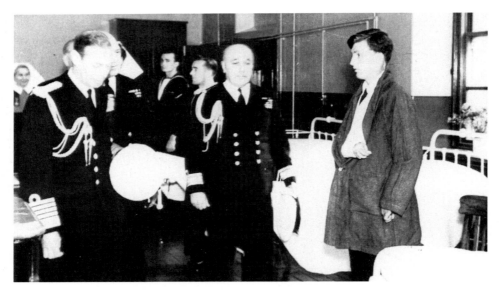

George VI also made a tour of inspection of the Royal Naval Hospital. Accompanied by Surgeon Rear Ad. C.E. Greeson, R.N., he is talking to a patient in one of the wards.

Right: The King taking leave of Surgeon Rear Ad. Greeson and Ad. Sir Harold Burrough, Commander-in-Chief the Nore. The King had taken tea with senior naval staff before leaving the hospital.

Below: Princess Marina, Duchess of Kent, inspecting a parade of more than 250 officers and ratings of the WRNS at Pembroke Barracks on 6 July 1953. The parade was held on the croquet lawn.

Left: Charles, Prince of Wales joined the Royal Navy in 1971. He is coming ashore from the Leander class frigate *Minerva*, on which he was serving, while the ship was based at Chatham.

Right: In February 1973, the *Minerva* sailed from Chatham Dockyard. Prince Charles was on deck working as a Fo'c'sle Officer, one of his duties as a naval Lieutenant. As *Minerva* left, a Royal Marine band on the quayside struck up the tune 'Charlie is my Darling'.

Prince Philip conversing with another group of dockyard employees during his December 1977 visit. He is talking to cleaner Jeanette Rogers, who is showing obvious delight at meeting the royal visitor.

Right: Princess Anne in the uniform of the Commander-in-Chief of the WRNS on her first visit to Chatham in June 1980. The Princess flew to the Navy Base and was greeted on her arrival by the Fleet Band of the Royal Marines playing a rendition of 'Annie's Song'.

Opposite below: Prince Philip was a career sailor until royal duties curtailed his life with the Senior Service. The Prince, wearing the uniform of an Admiral of the Fleet, visited the dockyard on 9 December 1977. He is seen sharing a joke with painter 'Gillie' Gambrill and other dockyard workers.

Princess Anne taking time during her visit to speak to a group of the relatives of naval personnel serving at Chatham.

Prince Charles is at Chatham in July 1981 for the rededication of the minesweeper *Bronington* which he had commanded before leaving the navy in 1977. He is speaking to a group of dockyard employees outside the Admiral's Office. This would be the last royal visit to the dockyard before its closure.

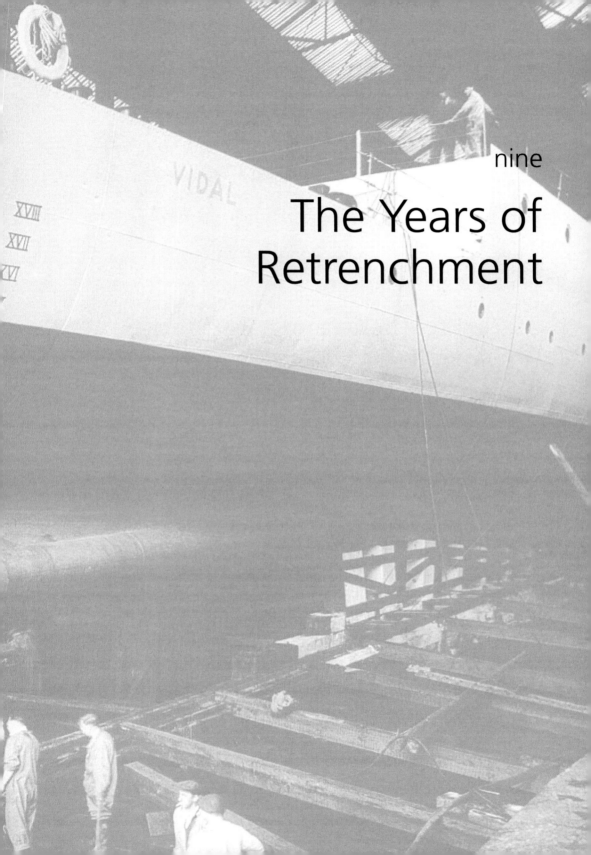

nine

The Years of Retrenchment

The return to peace in 1945 inevitably led to a rundown in the work levels at Chatham Dockyard. Those recruited to bolster up the workforce during the hostilities were discharged, including most of the 2,000-strong female workforce. Work for the established employees was at a premium, but care was taken to ensure that the great hardships which followed the First World War were not repeated, and discharges were kept to a minimum. To keep the workforce occupied, the yard was obliged to supplement its normal work with civilian contracts: the 'Dockyard Dustbins' would become part of dockyard folklore! The yard was kept ticking over, but was never again to witness that great hustle and bustle it had known during its heyday. The reduction in naval personnel and ships was also well in hand by 1950 when the Royal Marine Chatham Division was disbanded. Throughout the 1950s, one by one, outlying establishments were closed down as the progressive downsizing of the Royal Navy continued. In 1958 the Gun Wharf, comprising most of the site of the original Tudor dockyard, was sold. Sheerness, Chatham's sister dockyard at the mouth of the Medway, would close in the spring of 1960. During the following year the Royal Naval Hospital was transferred to the Ministry of Health on 15 January, while the Nore Command ceased to exist at the end of March, the Nore being relegated to a sub-command of Portsmouth.

The Clocktower Storehouse in 1946. The shrinking size of the navy would leave the dockyard with a surplus of storage space, resulting in the building being converted into necessary additional office accommodation.

The T-class submarine *Truculent* anchored in the Medway on 11 January 1950, while she was preparing to leave for machinery trials with seventy-nine naval and Chatham Dockyard personnel on board. Returning from a day's diving trials on the evening of the next day, she was struck and sunk in a collision with the Swedish tanker SS *Divina*.

Most of the men on board had survived the sinking of the *Truculent* but when, using escape apparatus, they arrived on the surface, no rescue vessels were in sight and the majority were swept down-channel to die from exposure. In all, sixty-four men were killed in the accident. Here, the salvage vessels are engaged in lifting the stricken submarine.

Following a major salvage operation the *Truculent* was raised on 14 March 1950. Patched and cleared of sea water she was again made buoyant before being towed into Sheerness Dockyard. In May she was sold to be broken up.

At the end of the Second World War a design team was set up in the dockyard to design and build a new diesel engine for the Royal Navy. The result was the Admiralty Standard Range 1 (ASR1) engine, one of which is shown here on completion of its construction in the dockyard factory.

The survey vessel *Vidal* was laid down in July 1950, and is shown here on No.7 Slip as she nears the end of her construction. She was the first vessel to use the ASR1 engine, and had two units to power each of her twin propellers.

The *Vidal*, last surface ship to be built in the dockyard, was launched on 31 July 1951. She was designed to carry a helicopter and, as she was expected to operate in all latitudes, was equipped with an air heating–cooling plant and extensive air conditioning.

On the evening of 4 December 1951 a column of some fifty young marine cadets was marching down Dock Road when a bus approached from behind. The driver, using only sidelights on the badly lit road, failed to see the cadets and ploughed his bus straight into the back of them. Twenty-four boys died as a result, and another eighteen were injured. This picture shows the scene in Dock Road on the morning following the tragedy.

The submarine *Talent* aground in the Medway with a salvage vessel in attendance, following an accident on the afternoon of 17 December 1954. She had been in No.3 Dock when the caisson sealing the entrance had given way, and the backwash of the inrush of water catapulted her out to ground on the mud at the opposite side of the river.

The replacement caisson for No.3 Dock, following its launch from No.7 Slip on 12 Februrary 1956. The *Talent* accident, which had left four dead, would result in new caissons being constructed for all of the dry docks.

The Gun Wharf storehouse, shortly before closure in 1958. The Gun Wharf was subsequently sold off. The northern part of the site would later be occupied by the large Lloyds office building, the remainder becoming a small council-owned park called 'Riverside'.

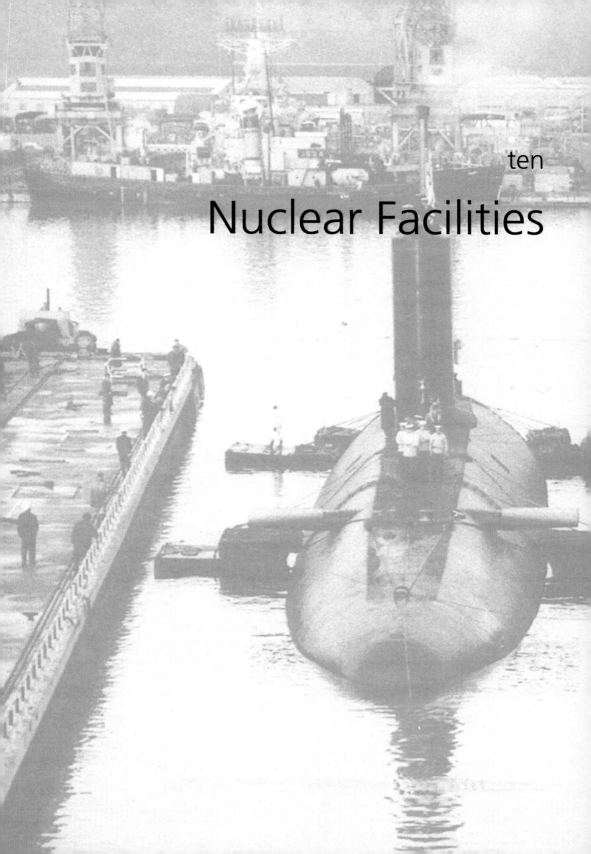

ten

Nuclear Facilities

Towards the end of 1966, Chatham Dockyard entered the atomic age when the nuclear powered submarine *Valiant* entered the yard and was docked in No.9 Dock. It had been decided to allocate the dockyard a new specialist rôle as a refitting base for fleet submarines; those that were nuclear powered but were conventionally armed with 21in homing torpedoes. On a site at the south side of No.1 Basin, incorporating Nos 6 and 7 docks, construction work had already begun to provide special docking, refuelling and refitting arrangements for nuclear submarine work. In 1967 the self-contained nuclear facilities complex became operational, containing two dry docks serviced by a huge cantilever crane, stores and workshops above and below ground, a ten-storey office block containing welfare facilities, marine accommodation, specialised buildings, mechanical and electrical plant, a boiler test house and an electrical sub-station, all enclosed within a restricted security area. The complex was officially opened by Vice-Ad. Sir Horace Law, Controller of the Navy, on 29 June 1968. A Nuclear Power Department was established in 1969 (prior to this a nuclear facilities section was responsible for the nuclear aspects of the dockyard's work). The future of the nuclear facilities complex was irrevocably tied to that of the dockyard as a whole. In 1981 it was announced that the yard was to be closed, and the nuclear department would not be excluded from its fate.

Opposite above: The *Valiant*, the first nuclear submarine to visit Chatham, entering the dockyard by the north lock on 12 December 1966. Earlier in the year, on 18 July, she had received her first commissioning. She would give her name to a class of submarines.

Opposite below: Architect's model of the nuclear facilities complex showing the two dry docks, supporting workshops, offices and other buildings, all dominated by the giant refuelling crane. The contractor was John Molem & Co. Ltd.

Below: The Health Physics Building. Here, the issue of anti-contamination clothing, monitoring of personnel for absorbed radiation levels, and other activities particular to protecting the health and safety of persons working on nuclear submarines.

Bottom: The refuelling crane, popularly referred to among dockyard employees as the hammerhead crane, was located between the two dry docks of the nuclear complex and, at 160ft high, formed one of the landmarks of the Medway Towns. It weighed 1,500 tons, and took nine months to erect.

The *Valiant* returned to Chatham in the summer of 1970 to became the first nuclear submarine to be refitted at the dockyard. She is arriving at No.6 Dock where her refit began in May 1970, taking two years to complete.

The first major refuelling refit of the Valiant-class submarine *Churchill* began at Chatham in December 1973. The work completed, she is seen at her recommissioning alongside No.7 Dock on 28 October 1975.

The *Churchill* being manoeuvred out of No.1 Basin by tugs. At times, during her refit, the workforce was employed around the clock seven days a week on shift work to ensure that she was completed on time.

The *Churchill* leaving Chatham by the north lock after her refit. When she first arrived at Chatham in April 1973, for a nine-week docking period the river Medway had to be dredged specifically to allow the submarine to gain access to the dockyard.

The *Conquerer* undergoing trials in dock during her refit. *Conquerer* completed her fifth and, to that date, fastest major nuclear refit, at Chatham in August 1977. Her refit took just ninety weeks to complete.

The *Conquerer* venting air as she floods her main ballast tanks to submerge during diving trials in No.1 Basin.

The *Conquerer* recommissioning in No.8 Dock, after her refit, in August 1977. The Band of the Royal Marines can be seen in the foreground and the ship's company in the background.

The *Valiant* returned to Chatham for her second refit in 1977. She is shown in No.6 Dock in June 1979, by which time the work of her refit was well advanced.

The *Valiant* towards the end of her refit, having emerged from the nuclear complex in order to carry out diving trials in No.1 Basin.

The *Warspite*, Valiant–class submarine, in No.7 Dock, undergoing her second refit in October 1981.

The *Dreadnought* alongside the basin at the nuclear facilities complex in 1979. Beyond her bows in No.7 Dock the *Warspite* is undergoing trials on her diesel-electric generators.

Tugs manoeuvring the *Warspite* in No.1 Basin at the beginning of 1982. Her refit was completed in March.

The *Churchill* when she was in No.6 Dock for her second refit at Chatham, which commenced in September 1980. She is almost totally obscured in this view, from November 1981, when the reactor access house was in place and her casing was covered in scaffolding and canvas awnings.

The *Churchill* in No.6 Dock as her long refit approaches its completion in 1982.

The *Churchill* recommissioning in No.6 Dock in 1982. She was the last submarine to be recommissioned at Chatham. On 23 May 1983 she emerged from the lock gates and headed down the Medway, thus bringing to a close the short era of the dockyard as a nuclear submarine refitting base.

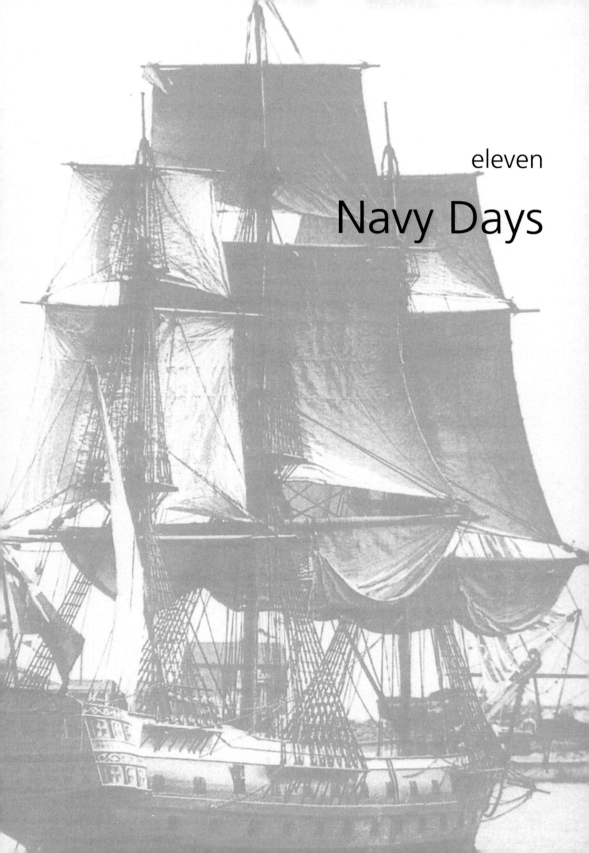

eleven

Navy Days

Chatham Navy Weeks were events during which the dockyard welcomed the general public through its gates to go aboard a variety of warships that were placed open to inspection, and to enjoy a number of displays, demonstrations and static exhibitions that were laid on for the visitors' entertainment. The first Navy Week took place in mid-August 1928. Thenceforth the Navy Weeks became an annual event until cancelled for the duration of the Second World War. With the return to peace the idea would be recommenced in 1948 as the annual Chatham Navy Days. From the naval perspective the Navy Days were a good public relations exercise, showing off the current hardware and giving insights into the various aspects of the work done by the Royal Navy and supporting services. They also presented useful opportunities for recruitment, giving encouragement to young men (and latterly women), particularly school leavers, who were considering taking up apprenticeships or other career opportunities in the dockyard or uniform branches of the Senior Service. All profits made during the Navy Days were paid into the funds of the Royal Navy and Royal Marine charities. By the second half of the twentieth century a succession of government defence economies had progressively diminished the size of the navy with the result that there was a noticeable reduction in the number of ships available for display at the Navy Days. The numbers would be partly made up by inviting some of the other countries of the NATO alliance to send along one or more of their ships to participate.

A commemorative postcard from the first Navy Week held in 1928. The event was a great success, drawing 42,000 visitors.

A souvenir card from the Chatham Navy Week of 1929. One of the basin displays on offer was a re-enactment entitled 'Manning and Arming of Boats to Capture an Arab Gun-running Dhow'.

Right: A model of the *Kent*, a frigate launched in 1762, on display during the 1929 Navy Week. The model, which was to a scale of one third full size, had been especially made for the event by naval ratings from the Barracks.

Below: The submarines L11 and L25 were among the numerous vessels on display for the 1929 Navy Week. Submarines were always one of the most popular attractions for the public with long queues forming to go on board.

Above: An anti–aircraft gun being demonstrated to visitors during the 1932 Navy Week.

Right: A souvenir cast-brass ashtray from the 1933 Navy Week. It was one of the more substantial of the various purchases available to the public as mementoes.

Official Guide to the 1935 Chatham Navy Week. By this time the Navy Weeks had become firmly established as a popular annual event.

Following the war the Navy Weeks were reborn as annual Navy Days. The events remained as popular as ever, which is evident here as visitors flock to inspect the various warships on display in No.3 Basin during a 1950s Navy Day.

The decks of the guided missile destroyer *Kent* thronging with members of the public during the 1964 Navy Days.

The Royal Marines' Motor Cycle Display Team was one of the attractions at the 1967 Navy Day.

The ships gathered at Chatham for the 1975 Navy Days are in this aerial view. The heavy repair ship *Triumph* (centre top) is alongside the northern wall in No.3 Basin.

Looking southwards across the entrance between Nos 2 and 3 Basins towards the bows of the frigates *Plymouth* and *Londonderry* in another aerial view from the 1975 Navy Days. The large building in the top right-hand corner is No.2 Electrical Shop.

OFFICIAL SOUVENIR PROGRAMME OF THE LAST

CHATHAM NAVY DAYS

MAY 30th & 31st 1982

THE FIRST

CANCELLED DUE TO
FALKLANDS CRISIS

THE LAST

THE FAMOUS

**ALL PROCEEDS GO
TO RN & RM
CHARITIES**

£1

The official programme prepared for the last Chatham Navy Days that would take place before the closure of the yard. Sadly, the event would be cancelled when an Argentinian invasion of the British Falkland Islands in the South Atlantic caused a crisis that would result in the Falklands War.

twelve

The Long Sunset

In 1956 the total reorganisation of the management structure of the dockyard was begun. The division of work by trade or profession was to be changed to a functional organisation with separate managers in charge of planning, personnel, yard services, finance, etc. On 1 June 1960 a personnel department was established to give a centralised authority to matters of employment and the welfare of employees. By the end of 1963 all of the other departments had also been set up under their respective managers. On 1 April 1964 the Admiralty was absorbed into the Ministry of Defence which in future would be responsible for administering all of the branches of the armed forces. The total reorganisation of the management structure and, in 1968, the opening of the nuclear complex with the subsequent formation of a nuclear department, brought a false hope among the employees that the dockyard was being guaranteed a long-term future. Before long there would be evidence of a different reality. By the 1970s the machinery of manufacture was quietly disappearing and the various workplaces began to take on an unaccustomed silence as fewer employees became engaged in actual production. In September 1971 the remaining naval establishments at Chatham were pulled together into a single administrative entity to be known as HM Naval Base. The final blow came on 25 June 1981 when the Secretary of State for Defence announced in the House of Commons that the navy base was to close. The official closure on 31 March 1984 would bring an end to almost four-and-a-half centuries of royal naval presence in the Medway.

Main Office Building, erected to house the new Planning and Finance Managers' Departments, formed as part of the reorganisation of the management structure in the early 1960s.

The rear of the Main Office Building, the bridge across the road linking it to the Mould Loft and Drawing Office building, now part of the Planning Manager's Department.

Mould Loft Floor, situated on the upper storey of the Mould Loft Building, had become greatly under-employed as Chatham abandoned its role as a shipbuilding yard. The mock-up of a submarine in wood is on the right.

The factory was the biggest engineering workshop in the dockyard with a floor area of 6.5 acres. It remained the largest single place of work for the dockyard workforce, though with numbers considerably less than in the heyday of the dockyard when it employed around 600 men.

The frigate *Exmouth* commenced a two-year conversion at Chatham in 1966 to become the world's first warship to be powered exclusively by gas turbine plant. She was fitted with a Rolls-Royce Marine Olympus engine to act as a booster unit, and two Rolls-Royce Proteus Engines for cruise conditions. Thus powered, the *Exmouth* could achieve 28 knots.

The figurehead of Ad. Lord Nelson ablaze on 12 July 1966 when the historic No.2 Slip was burnt down. A line of other figureheads, displayed alongside the slip, were also lost in the blaze. Fourteen fire engines attended the fire which was started through horseplay by an apprentice.

A figurehead that remained, occupying a prominent position near the Main Gate, was that of the *Wellesley*, which had seventy-four guns and was launched at Bombay in 1815. Having served as a guard ship at Chatham in the 1860s, she spent her later years as a training ship at Purfleet. Reclaimed by the Admiralty on 23 September 1940, she was hit during an air raid on the following day and sunk.

Above: A Sea Vixen, transported from Gosport, being unloaded by floating crane from the Royal Fleet Auxiliary vessel *Robert Middleton*, in No.3 Basin on 21 July 1968.

Right: The aircraft was reloaded onto the RFA vessel *Bacchus* to be conveyed out to the Far East. RFA vessels were the work horses of the navy, playing a vital role in carrying stores and equipment to wherever they were required around the globe.

Above: The *Diamond*, Daring Class Destroyer, in No.5 Dock for repair in 1969. She was built in 1952 and was approaching the end of her active life, but was not finally scrapped until 1981.

Left: The *Opossum* in No.2 Dock, following the commencement of her refit in 1970. She had originally been launched at the Cammel Laird shipyard in Birkenhead on 23 May 1963.

The frigate *Yarmouth* arrived at the dockyard for repairs on 15 March 1972, having damaged her bow in collision with an Icelandic gunboat during the Cod War.

The frigate *Hermione* in No.9 Dock undergoing a three-year-long refit and modernisation programme, including a Seawolf missile conversion.

The *Hermione* leaving Chatham on 21 June 1983. She was the last ship to leave Chatham before closure and was ceremonially escorted downriver by a small flotilla of dockyard vessels, the Flag Officer Medway aboard his barge leading the way.

No.2 Dock at the beginning of 1984. Effectively the dockyard was dead. The ships had gone, leaving the docks and basins empty and the workshops silent. There was no sign of human activity. For practical purposes the yard shut on 30 September 1983 when, as a Royal Marine band played 'Sunset', the Flag Officer Medway's flag was lowered for the last time. The official closure at the end of March was that of an already abandoned dockyard.

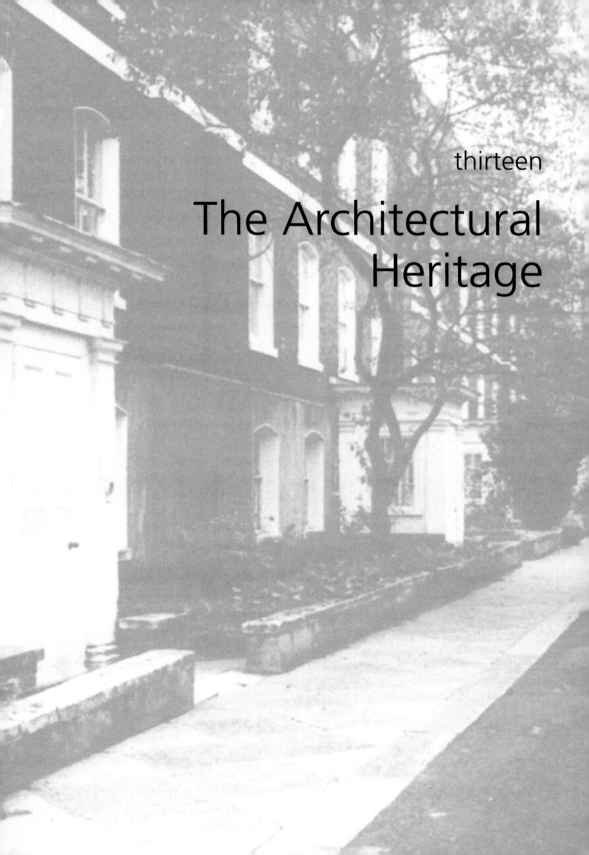

thirteen

The Architectural Heritage

The closure of Chatham Dockyard in 1984 left behind a remarkable range of preserved historic buildings that represented a complete Georgian and early Victorian Royal Dockyard. This preponderance of architectural heritage lay clustered in the 80 acres of the older, southerly section of the yard. Included in the wide array of structures were the Main Gate, Dockyard church, the many workshops, storehouses, domestic accommodation and office buildings, plus the three dry docks, five covered slipways and a mast pond. Also extant, at the southern extremity of the yard, were the eighteenth-century ropery buildings. Within the enclave, Brunel's Saw Mills, the North Mast Pond and the Boat Store remained as memorials to the nation's great maritime past. The large Victorian extension that lay northwards of the more ancient areas of the yard also contained some notable architectural features, not least of which were the three large basins – the most westerly one possessing five stone-built dry docks. The imposing pumping station for the docks stood as a monument to Victorian ingenuity. Adjacent to the four dry docks on the southern side of the basins were the Factory, Boiler Shop and No.8 Machine Shop, three substantial early Victorian structures which originated from Woolwich Dockyard, having been dismantled and then reassembled at Chatham when the Thameside Dockyard closed in 1869.

Above: Upnor Castle facing the dockyard from the opposite bank of the Medway is the only building to have survived from the Tudor period. It was completed in 1564 to protect the anchorage and yard from attack, but it would be a century before it was called upon to meet the challenge, exchanging fire with the Dutch during the raid of 1667.

Left: The Main Gate was completed in 1720. The twin towers originally provided accommodation for the porter and the boatswain of the yard. The coat of arms of George III is above the arch.

The Police Offices, a single-storey structure erected as a Guardhouse in 1764. The colonnade, its ten Ionic columns made out of wood, was added in 1813.

The Dockyard church, a rectangular building of yellow stock brick with a bell cote above its southern end, was designed by Edward Holl, Surveyor of Buildings to the Admiralty, and completed in 1810.

The Dockyard church interior. The altar and original box pews are seen from the tiered gallery.

The Dockyard church interior looking towards rear of church. Cast-iron columns support the gallery. The coat of arms are those of George III. The last service at the church was held on Christmas Eve, 1981.

The Sail Loft, built in 1734. It was given three storeys, the lower two being used for the storage of canvas and finished sails, while the upper storey was the sail floor, designed to have no supporting columns to interfere with the laying out of large sails. For many years part of the building was given over as a Colour Loft, manufacturing flags for the Royal Navy.

The Cashier's Office. Originally a single-storey late eighteenth-century building, the upper storey was added during the period 1810–1820. John Dickens, father of the famous author Charles, served as a clerk in this building between 1817 and 1823. Latterly it served as 'The Office of the Technical Staff; Flag Officer, Medway'.

Naval Terrace. An elegant terrace of twelve houses built between 1722 and 1731 in order to accommodate the senior officials of the dockyard.

The Commisioner's House, latterly known as Medway House. This fine building with a large eaved cornice and well spaced windows was constructed in 1703, when the newly appointed Resident Commissioner, George St Lo, put in a formal request for a more substantial building to be provided as his residence.

The Admiral's Offices. The building, designed by Edward Holl, was erected in 1808 in order to house the offices of the Dockyard Commissioner and his staff.

The Clock Tower building. Originally constructed in 1723, it housed the Mold Loft floor on its upper storey until 1755. The left-hand six ground-floor bays were open and used as saw pits. Refurbished in 1803, the building served as a storehouse for most of its working life before eventually being used as an annexe to the Admiral's Offices.

No.3 Slipway, the oldest and most southerly of the line of five adjacent covered slipways. It had spent the latter part of its working life as a storage area.

The contiguous row of covered slipways seen from across the North Mast Pond. From left to right: the partly obscured No.3 Slip, Nos 4, 5 and 6 Slips, completed with metal roofs in 1847 then the large No.7 slipway completed in 1855.

The Lower Boathouse which was built around 1844. It is seen looking northwards across the North Mast Pond, which was dug in 1702.

Above: The Saw Mill, completed in 1814 to the designs of Marc Brunel. It later found new use as the dockyard laundry. Between 1943 and 1960 it also housed a group training centre for the electrical fitter apprentices.

Right: The southern end of the yard. Anchor Wharf with its long line of naval storehouses and, at the rear, the double roof of the 1792 ropery can be seen.

Above: Looking south along Anchor Wharf with its two huge naval storehouses. The closest was completed in 1796. Its northern end was used as a Rigging House. Beyond its southern end stands the second storehouse which is nearly 700ft long and finished in 1785.

Left: Viewed from a fixed laying machine, dating from 1856 and still in use for manufacturing rope, the laying floor of the quarter-mile-long ropery stretches out into the distance.

fourteen

Life After Death

Upon the closure of the navy base in 1984, its site would be broken up into three large zones. The first of these, incorporating the southern and oldest part of the former dockyard, and containing the majority of its most historic buildings and structures, was vested by the government in an independent charity, the Chatham Historic Dockyard Trust, to be preserved as a heritage site, and a one-off grant of £11.3 million was made for its future care and maintenance. It has since been progressively developed as a tourist venue, with a visitor centre being created in the former Galvanising Shop. The Ropery has continued to operate in private hands and the vast northern storehouse at Anchor Wharf now contains a large museum of dockyard artefacts. Today the historic dockyard is one of Britain's major tourist attractions and has been granted world heritage site status. The second zone was passed to English Estates to be developed as residential and commercial accommodation. It contained the greater part of St Mary's Island, Nos 1 and 2 Basins, and the nuclear facilities complex. It also included the site and buildings of the former naval barracks, now mainly occupied as a campus for the University of Greenwich. The final zone, containing No.3 Basin and the lock gates at Bull's Nose, was taken over by the Medway Dock Company for utilisation as a commercial port. Trade has gradually increased in the docks since their opening and the trend is predicted to continue now that direct access to the national motorway network has become available via the Medway Tunnel.

Above: In the Chatham Historic Dockyard the former Mast House from 1755 has been fully renovated. Today it houses the Wooden Walls Exhibition which presents, in the form of a series of tableaux, the working life of a mid-eighteenth century dockyard worker.

Left: The sloop *Gannet*, launched at Sheerness Dockyard in 1878, was brought to the historic dockyard in 1988 and, having undergone extensive restoration in No.4 Dock, is now open to visitors.

The *Ocelot* was, in 1962, the last submarine to be built at Chatham for the Royal Navy. Completed in 1964, she remained in service until 1981. She was brought back to the former dockyard and placed on permanant display in July 1992.

The C-class destroyer *Cavalier*, a Second World War veteran from 1944. Paid off at Chatham in 1972, she was back in 1998, being placed in No.2 Dock for conservation as a subsequent tourist attraction.

Above left: A commemorative stone has for many years been set at the head of No.2 Dock, informing passers-by that the dock was the site of the building of the *Victory*, launched in 1765, and destined as the flagship of Admiral Horatio Nelson to become most illustrious ship in the Royal Navy.

Above right: Although the original *Victory* is now preserved at Portsmouth, a large model of her is to be seen in the Chatham Historic Dockyard Museum. It was made for *That Hamilton Woman*, a cinematic production from 1941 by Alexander Korda which was Winston Churchill's favourite film.

Looking from the east across the northern area of the former dockyard now possessed by English Estates and Medway Ports Ltd. In the top left corner the dual carriageway of the road to the new Medway Tunnel passes between the old Naval Barracks and dockyard, before vanishing under the river. In the opposite corner, on St Mary's Island, there is now a large housing development.

No.1 Basin now serves as a yacht marina, also used for small boat sailing. The original entrance from the Medway was filled in during the 1930s but has now been reinstated, providing convenient access to the two western basins.

Opposite below: New housing, part of a 9-acre development within the historic dockyard, which would cause disappointed conservationists to claim that the Chatham Historic Trust had reneged on assurances that any new building would be compatible with the historic environment.

New houses now front the northern side of No.2 Basin, part of the conversion by English Estates of the majority of St Mary's Island into a large housing estate.

The eastern end of the Medway Tunnel where it emerges into the site of the old dockyard, now cut into two sections by the dual carriageway of the feeder road.

No.3 Basin is now the hub of a compact but thriving commercial port operated by Medway Ports Ltd. As docks, the basin can accommodate vessels of up to 26ft draft. Eight berthing spaces have been created along a total wharfage of over 1,300 yards.

One of the many merchant vessels now to be seen in the docks is in No.6 Berth. Although the docks are used by a variety of companies, a large portion of the trade is currently with paper and other forest products. The docks now handle over a million tons of cargo a year.

If you are interested in purchasing other books published by The History Press,
or in case you have difficulty finding any of our books in your local bookshop,
you can also place orders directly through our website
www.thehistorypress.co.uk